IDEAS IN PSYCHOANALYSIS

Eros

G000039065

Nicola Abel-Hirscn

Series editor: Ivan Ward

ICON BOOKS UK

TOTEM BOOKS USA

Published in the UK in 2001
by Icon Books Ltd., Grange Road,
Duxford, Cambridge CB2 4QF
E-mail: info@iconbooks.co.uk
www.iconbooks.co.uk

Published in the USA in 2001
by Totem Books
Inquiries to: Icon Books Ltd.,
Grange Road, Duxford
Cambridge CB2 4QF, UK

Sold in the UK, Europe, South Africa
and Asia by Faber and Faber Ltd.,
3 Queen Square, London WC1N 3AU
or their agents

Distributed to the trade in the USA
by National Book Network Inc.,
4720 Boston Way, Lanham,
Maryland 20706

Distributed in the UK, Europe,
South Africa and Asia by
Macmillan Distribution Ltd.,
Houndmills, Basingstoke RG21 6XS

Distributed in Canada by
Penguin Books Canada,
10 Alcorn Avenue, Suite 300,
Toronto, Ontario M4V 3B2

Published in Australia in 2001
by Allen & Unwin Pty. Ltd.,
PO Box 8500, 83 Alexander Street,
Crows Nest, NSW 2065

ISBN 1 84046 276 0

Typesetting by Hands Fotoset

Printed and bound in the UK by
Cox & Wyman Ltd., Reading

Eros: 'A Principle of Attraction'[1]

Eros is the idea of a force which 'binds together' the elements of human existence – physically through sex, emotionally through love and mentally through imagination.

In Freud's time, talk of sex, particularly the sexual wishes and phantasies of children, was shocking to many of his contemporaries. But what would shock us today? An idea explored here is that one cannot have the binding of intercourse (sexual, emotional or intellectual intercourse) without a form of love. You can of course have sexual penetration without love – paedophilia is a reminder of that – but this is not the same as an intercourse. The form of love necessary for intercourse is understood to be the two-way recognition of the difference of the other, separate from the subject, existing in his or her own life and each an object of concern to the other. Without this, there is no 'two' to be bound in intercourse with each other.[2]

I take my starting point from Freud's concept of 'life instinct', which he calls 'Eros'. Prior to his introduction of Eros, Freud placed a key emphasis on sexuality as the source of motivation and energy in many activities, whether overtly sexual or not. When he introduced the concept of Eros, he included sexuality in it, but also added the notion of a general principle of attraction. Eros, he said, is what binds things together – and, one could add, binds them together in a way that leads to something alive or new.

Beyond the Pleasure Principle

In the middle years of his life, and against a backdrop of war and the death of his daughter Sophie, Freud wrote what he describes as a highly speculative paper. 'Beyond the Pleasure Principle' (1920) is an exploration of life and death, conceptualised by Freud in terms of 'instincts'. Freud has interesting questions to ask, such as: What brings things to life? Has death been there from the beginning of life? He turns to biology and makes use of his findings in thinking about the dynamics of the mind. He reaches the view that 'life instinct', or Eros, 'holds all living things together'.[3] In later works, he further comments that it 'form[s] living substance into ever greater unities, so that life may be prolonged and brought to higher development'[4] and, again, that it 'aims at complicating life and at the same time, of course, at preserving it'.[5]

One piece of biological research that caught his attention was work on 'vital differences'. The research studied cells which come together and then separate again. The cells are rejuvenated by this process. Freud suggests that whilst organisms generally aim for a release of tension, which leads eventually to death (see 'A Note on Thanatos' below), at the same time

[U]nion with the living substance of a different

5

*individual increases those tensions, intro-
ducing what may be described as fresh 'vital
differences' which must then be lived off.*[6]

Freud saw this conjugation of cells as the
forerunner of sexual reproduction in higher
creatures involving, as we now know, the
recombination of genetic material. Freud's
view is of a live process in which 'bringing
together' has a disruptive but rejuvenating
effect on the elements or parties involved.
Eros is a *tension* in the organism.

There is an interesting contemporary question
in this context to do with the difference between
cloning and reproduction. Both processes
result in a life. Cloning, however, leads to a
repetition of something that is already there.
By contrast, in sexual reproductive activity,
although foreign bodies are generally taken by
the immune system to be a threat to life, the
body has to encounter – and be host to – first
the sperm and then the developing embryo.

In his or her emotional/mental life, a person can react like an immune system repelling foreign experience or ideas. In order for sexual, emotional or mental intercourse to be possible, the 'foreignness' or difference of the other person or idea has to be entertained. Part of the difficulty in doing this is that difference involves the recognition that the other person has things one does not have oneself. The other sex, for example, has a body with different sexual characteristics. At the same time, difference holds the promise of something new and is the necessary condition for intercourse (between different parties) – be this sexual, emotional or intellectual.

Sex and Love

With his concept of Eros, Freud introduces new ground to his overriding interest in the sexual instincts. Eros provides the potential for a unified theory of sex and love in which neither is secondary to the other and both are forms of a 'binding together' or intercourse between different elements. Freud does not develop his ideas on Eros himself, and is perhaps more interested in the idea of 'death instinct'. Nevertheless, Freud's Eros can be developed today, particularly in relation to Melanie Klein's innovative work on love, and the work of Wilfred Bion and others on imagination. However, to go back a step, first I want to illustrate the problems that arise if sex and love are kept separate from each other. This happens in a curious way in psychoanalytic theory itself when a rather simplistic opposition is set up between the theory of Freud (Instinct Theory) and that of Klein and others (Object Relations Theory).

'Instincts' and 'Relations'

Firstly: **Instinct Theory** – a caricature of this can be seen in the view that men only want sex. In this view, the appetite for sex arises within the person. The person then looks for someone to satisfy their need. What matters is the sex rather than the person who offers it.

Secondly: **Object Relations Theory** – a caricature of this can be seen in the view that women only want love. In this view, all that matters is the emotional relationship. There appear to be no sexual desires arising in the woman.

In both these caricatures, there is a split between sex and love. In the first, the relation-ship with the other person is a means to get sex. In the second, sex for the woman is a means to get love.

In fact, if one splits sex and love like this, it could be argued that what one gets is neither sex nor love. Sex without recognition of, and concern for, the other person cannot be an intimacy between *two* people. Likewise, the love in the caricature above of Object Rel-ations Theory seems more like a wish for security or flattery than a desire to be with the other person. This is not to say that the quantity and quality of love in an affair would be the same as, say, that in a long-standing marriage, but that a concern for the other as other (cf. love) makes intercourse between two different people possible. In the same way, in relation to love, the way sex is expressed is very different between lovers or, say, mothers and babies, but something is arguably missing if the mother–baby relationship is devoid of anything sensual.

With this in mind, it seems better to try to hold the two theories together (Instinct and Object Relations) and draw on both. In contrast to Klein and other object-relations analysts, Freud places greater emphasis on sex than on love, but his concept of Eros can encompass their understanding of love, as well as more recent work by Bion and others on the imagination.

A Note on Thanatos[7]

From the time of his 'speculative paper'

'Beyond the Pleasure Principle', Freud held to the view that conflict between life and death instinct lay at the heart of life. In his view, death instinct, which he called 'Thanatos', is the opposite to Eros. It aims at death either through reducing differentiation and silently pulling the organism back into an inorganic state, or through active destruction. Innate, the instinct is initially turned on the self; it is then deflected onto the outside world as aggression.

Freud conceived of Eros and Thanatos as having a multitude of differing relations with each other. He thought, for example, that eating involves both instincts, one in the destruction of the object eaten and the other in the intent through eating to live. Another example is sexual intercourse, in which aggression is put together with the most intimate unity.

A great deal has been written about Freud's concept of death instinct. One question in particular relates to whether aggression is always to do with the death instinct. In contemporary psychoanalysis, a convincing view is to see 'life instinct' and 'death instinct' as two masters. The question then ceases to be, 'Is aggression death instinct?' and becomes, 'Is aggression being used, in this particular instance, to serve life or to serve death?'

Eros in the Body: What is Sexuality?

Much has been written on sexuality. My focus here is going to be on sexuality from the point of view of Eros.

Eros 'Form[s] Living Substance into ever Greater Unities'[8]

In Freud's model of sexuality,[9] we start off at the level of the infant with what he calls 'polymorphous perverse' sexuality. By this, he means that infantile sexuality, whilst it may involve excitement felt in the genitals, is more like the sexuality seen in adult foreplay (for which it is the precursor). All kinds of parts of the body can become sexually stimulated. In particular, as a part of the body becomes a general focus for the infant and child, it also becomes a focus of sexual excitement. Initially, the infant concentrates on feeding – involving the mouth and the nipple and the act of sucking. This, Freud delineates as the 'Oral phase' in the development of the child's sexuality. The second phase is the 'Anal phase' and is connected with the child's focus on its bowels and toilet-training. Freud thought that this was followed by what he termed the 'Phallic phase'. This phase in particular has been controversial, as some think that it does not give a picture of the development of the girl's sexuality and that it is an attack on women to define their sexuality in relation to their absence of a penis. It does seem that there are real problems with this phase, but perhaps what can be said here is that the Phallic phase has in it the idea of the hatred (as well as attraction) of difference. The other sex has what one does not.

Freud argues that in adolescence and adulthood the diverse strands of sexuality (for example, from different erotogenous zones like the mouth, anus, skin and genitals) become united and focused on genitality.

Although Freud does not explicitly liken this model of 'binding diverse strands into a complex whole' to the same factor in his model of Eros, they are very much alike, and it may be that the sexual model informed his emphasis on this in Eros.

The binding together of 'diverse strands' of sexuality is dependent on the recognition of vital differences, particularly the difference between the sexes and that between the generations (between parents and children).

Eros, Sexuality and 'Vital Difference': Two Children's Phantasies

One seven-year-old girl, after spending many weeks experimenting with weeing like a boy (standing up over the toilet), asked her mother if sex was people weeing on each other. She seemed content at that point with the answer 'no' and did not ask what, if not weeing, sex then was. The impression she gave was that accurate information about sex (information to which she had access) was not what mattered at this point, she would work it out in her own time. She may also have been feeling anxious about the idea of penetration in intercourse.

It would not be right, I think, to say that the little girl wanted to be a boy. It seemed more that she wanted to be both a boy and a girl, and in her model of intercourse both can do the same thing – wee on each other. Her model of sexual intercourse – weeing – is also something she was physically capable of doing herself in 'intercourse' with her father, or 'as a boy' with her mother.

At this point in the young girl's development, the difference between the sexes and the difference between the generations is held at bay.

By contrast, in a dream from her sister who is two years older, we do see a differentiation, and an excited one at that, between boys and girls. In the dream, the girl was with her friend in the girls' toilet at school. Each was in a neighbouring toilet-booth and each had the door open. Two boys from their class came in. The girl quickly closed her door. She allayed her own worries about having been seen with the thought that the other girl's door was still open and she would certainly have been seen.

Then the girl was in the seaside resort she visited every year with her family. The resort is on the Atlantic and has the large rolling waves of a surfing beach. There are seals in the water. In the dream, the girl is out in deep water waiting for a wave she can surf on. She cannot see her family, but they are around her in the sea. She is then 'picked up' by the wave and flung across the water. It was, she said on telling the dream, like flying.

If the child were in analysis, then one would

have her thoughts about the dream and other analytic material to help in understanding it. Without this, what follows is more speculative.

In the child's mind, it is possible that 'seeing' genitals is to do with having sex, and that toilets appear in the dream not just because that is actually where the children might 'see' each other at school, but because the child connects defecation with sex and babies.

Faeces are the first thing a child produces. Faecal material is his or hers and it can be either given as a gift or withheld by the child. To give up the equation of faeces and baby – to realise that they are not produced in the same way – can be hard for the child, because it involves an admission to herself that she is small, and not able to have father's babies as mother can. The child is of a *different* generation to the parents.

What of the ocean in the dream? It would seem to be a sense of an exciting and expansive force that can take her over and support her at the same time. Anyone who has ridden a wave to shore, had an orgasm, fallen in love or felt an idea coming to life knows that all four are the same kind of experience. In each case, a moment of mobility is granted – to body, feelings or mind.

The dream conveys something of the conflicts the child might feel in relation to her emerging sexuality, and may itself be a way of trying to work on these. In particular, the conflict between wanting to be 'seen' by a boy (and eventually 'entered' by a man) and the anxiety or shame felt about this.

In the Oedipal situation, to which I now turn, it is in phantasy that the child can put sex and love together in the desired relationship with mother or father. In adulthood, if one's sexual partner can be known to be different from one's infantile phantasy world, then the kind of complexity of wishes and feelings seen in the child's dream can add depth to the new adult relationship.

Oedipus: Incestuous Desire and its Resolution

Many people will have come across the story of Oedipus, and numerous papers have been written on it in psychoanalysis and other disciplines. Freud commented on the capacity of this story to fascinate, and it has continued to do so even when more of its unconscious content (the wish to kill one parent and marry the other) is consciously known by today's post-Freud audience.

A brief sketch of the myth, portrayed in the plays of Sophocles, is as follows. Laius, the father of Oedipus, is warned by an oracle that his son will kill him and marry his wife. In the film *Edipo Re* (1960), directed by Pier Paolo Pasolini, one sees a young father jealous of his baby, Oedipus. The baby has mother's attention and the breast is for milk and therefore not sexually available to the father. Whether or not jealousy of the child is involved, the oracle is believed and the baby is pierced by a brooch in the ankles and left to die on a desolate hillside. Oedipus (the name means 'swollen feet') is, however, saved and grows up believing himself to be the son of a neighbouring king. He then hears of the prophecy himself and leaves the people he believes to be his parents in order to protect them from the threatened murderous violence towards his father and seduction of his mother. On his travels, he comes to a cross-roads where he has to jump for his life out of the way of a fast-moving carriage. His rage boils over and he kills the man in the carriage, who in fact is his natural father. He arrives in Thebes (his birth home, although he does not know it), where he encounters the Sphinx, who sets him the following riddle:

What is that which has one voice and yet becomes four-footed and two-footed and three-footed?[10]

(Apollodorus, *The Library*, 3.5.7–9)

The answer to the riddle is man, who in the course of his life first crawls, then walks and ends up with a walking-stick. Oedipus answers correctly. The Sphinx, as a consequence of his correct answer, kills itself.

Creon, the current king of Thebes, has offered the kingdom and the hand of Jocasta, Laius's widow, to whoever can solve the riddle. Oedipus, apparently unwittingly, marries his mother and they have children. Oedipus then discovers that he is the murderer of the previous King and further, that it is his birth-father that he has murdered. He has murdered his father and married his mother as the oracle predicted. When Jocasta discovers the truth, she kills herself; Oedipus blinds himself. The corruption of relations between parents and children is repeated when Oedipus himself is unable to take care of his own children. He puts on one of his sons a 'curse of strife' which he describes as a continuation of the curse on Laius.

Freud thought that the play portrayed a dynamic that is every child's wish: namely, to marry one parent and murder the other. He gave as an example the Freud family nanny's dream that his wife (her mistress) had died and she then married Freud. Through his self-analysis, he found the same constellation in himself.[11] Freud emphasised the child's wish to marry the parent of the opposite sex, but both Freud and psychoanalysts since have thought that the child experiences a hetero-sexual and a homosexual version of the same wish, with the parent of the opposite sex and the parent of the same sex respectively. The young girl above, who asked if sex was people weeing on each other, seems to want the possibility of both versions. She wanted to be like her father, and wee on mother, and at other times was very intent on 'marrying' father.

What might lead the child to give up these incestuous phantasies? Freud thought that little boys feared a retaliatory castration by the excluded father. The story he gives for the little girl is less clear. Klein thought that the equivalent fear for the girl was that her phantasied attacks on mother will lead to a reprisal by mother.

The violence of the feared castration or retaliation echoes the violence in the myth of Oedipus which is strikingly lacking in love. Parents abandon their baby to die. There is no possibility of repairing violent acts or even 'mistakes'. Instead, people kill or blind themselves. As an adult man, Oedipus is unable to love his son.

Recent work in psychoanalysis, however, has looked more closely at the place of love in the Oedipal situation and, in particular, love for the one who is 'left out'. This is love for the parent the child wishes to exclude, in order to have a passionate relationship with the other parent. Love for the excluded one can become a sympathetic love of the child for itself too, excluded from the parental relationship. Freud (and this was much developed by Klein after him) suggests that this form of love is a factor in children giving up or repressing incestuous desires.

Parents, of course, can help or hinder in these things. In particular, sexual intrusion by a parent can inhibit and damage a child's sexual and general development. It may also be that the parents are not together and that one or other is not available to the child. This would clearly affect the child, but internal processes are also strong and a child can have a concept of a parental couple even if the external reality is different from this.

If the child is able to leave the parents alone – literally and in the child's mind – the parental relationship becomes a template for allowing 'intercourse' to occur. The child may, for example, be enabled to allow ideas to come together in his or her own mind, instead of having to rigidly control what he or she thinks.

To be excluded from the 'exciting' and 'mysterious' relationship of the parents and feel small and unknowing as a child might, are, however, difficult experiences. In some people, there is a great wish to avoid the experience of generational difference and continue in the illusion that one is really the erotic partner of the parent. The price paid for this, however, is that one loses the chance for real physical or psychic intercourse with a new partner. This was the case for Anna O.

Anna O: The Avoidance of 'Vital Difference'[12]

Anna O's real name was Bertha Pappenheim. She was a friend of Freud's wife and was in treatment with Joseph Breuer, Freud's early mentor and colleague.

The psychoanalyst Ronald Britton argues that Anna O was unable to give up the illusion of her father as her partner, and enacted this relation with Breuer. Britton comments that

Freud heard two versions of the story of Anna O's treatment with Breuer. One was the official version, the other was told one summer evening when the two men dined alone.

When she entered treatment with Breuer, Anna O was 21. On the surface of things, she was very eligible, but according to Breuer had never had a romantic attachment or any sexual thoughts. During the time she had nursed her dying father, Anna became progressively weaker and developed anorexia. She acquired a severe cough, a squint, various paralyses and suffered a loss of normal speech. At the same time, two distinct states of consciousness established themselves. In one, she was melancholy and anxious but relatively normal. In the other, she hallucinated and misbehaved.

Breuer gave an attentive interest to her symptoms and states of mind. He became the only person she would recognise and he also became the only person who could feed her. When he was there, she became euphoric; when he was away, she became much worse. Britton notes that Breuer did not seem to connect her states of mind to her attachment to him.

Britton takes up the story himself on the basis of new evidence provided more recently by the historian of psychoanalysis Henri Ellenberger.[13] Breuer's wife appears to have been angry and impatient with his involvement with Anna O. Britton suggests that Anna O was hospitalised for a few days from 7 June 1881 as a consequence of Frau Breuer's insistence that her husband spend more time with her. The Breuers left for a few days, and during that month their daughter was conceived.

Exactly one year later, Anna O's treatment ended with her enactment of two extraordinary scenes. The first scene was reported in the official story, the second scene was not.

The first scene involves a hallucination Anna O had suffered whilst nursing her father. She and Breuer appeared to believe this to be the key to her illness, now expiated through the enactment and cured. The second scene happened shortly afterwards:

After leaving Anna O for the last time Breuer was called back to find her confused and writhing with abdominal cramps. Asked what was the matter, she replied, 'Now comes Dr Breuer's child'. Freud commented 'at that moment Breuer held the key in his hand but he dropped it'. In conventional horror he took flight and left the patient to a colleague.[14]

Britton argues that Anna O had the (unconscious) belief that she was in her father's bedroom not as a daughter/nurse, but as his partner. The union is a deadly one, as she starves herself to death with him, but it is nonetheless a union. Anna O then repeated her belief with her new doctor. Instead of being Breuer's patient, she is his partner – and an exciting and interesting partner at that. In phantasy, she has his child. It seems that Breuer could not let himself see this – perhaps he felt he was implicated in her feelings for him; he certainly did not know what to do with them. Freud, by contrast, was able to be curious about what had happened.

A Concluding Note on Sexuality

Freud's concept of Eros as 'binding' into more complex wholes focuses attention on how diverse strands are drawn together in the development of a person's sexuality. It is a complex model of sexuality, and can accommodate individuals' different sexual development. Further to this, whilst Freud's emphasis on genitality may contain elements of moral judgement, it is firmly based on his recognition of the link between intercourse and new life. This is self-evident when it comes to human procreation, but the importance of intercourse as a model goes much further than this.

Even in relation to sexuality, intercourse may not be literal and could be an alive intimacy between two people. What would not be intercourse from the point of view of Eros, even if it involved penetration, would be those situations where another person's body is just used for sex (this is really a form of masturbation) or where a rigid, sadistic or dismissive control is exerted over the other person and their separateness and difference denied. This is not to say, of course, that sexuality does not have aggression in it. The distinction is between aggression as part of an intercourse and aggression used to avoid or destroy an alive interchange.

Eros in the Emotions: What is Love?

In relation to sexuality, love and thought, there is a difference between seeing the relationship between oneself and the other as one would wish it to be, and on the other hand discovering what *it* really is. In 'love', this is broadly the difference between idealised love and a more complex and generous love. Idealised love is the way love often starts, and it tends towards a partial and wish-fulfilling picture of both the other and oneself. There may be little awareness of difference or the idealisation of it. As with assumptions in thought (which I move on to later), idealised love is notorious for ignoring evidence that contradicts it. At the same time, unless it has to be held onto in a rigid way, idealisation can 'melt' as one begins to find out about the other person. One's love can then become something more complex and generous: complex because it involves a recognition of more aspects of the personality, including uncomfortable or unpleasant ones; generous because it involves a recognition of the other person in his or her own right, and a concern about them.

Idealised Love

My face in thine eye, thine in mine appeares,
And true plaine hearts doe in the faces rest,
Where can we finde two better hemispheares
Without sharpe North, without declining
  West?
What ever dyes, was not mixt equally;
If our two loves be one, or, thou and I
Love so alike, that none doe slacken, none
  can die.[15]

  (John Donne, 'The Good-Morrow')

Freud thought it part of the essential nature of falling in love to idealise the loved person. People, he suggests, would not be so foolish as to fall in love if they had their eyes properly open to the strengths and weaknesses of the loved one. Love is an everyday madness – a point recognised by the seventeenth-century playwright William Congreve, when he wrote:

If this be not love, then it is madness, and then it is pardonable.[16]

(William Congreve, *The Old Bachelor*)

Along with the idealisation of the loved person, Freud thought that people saw an idealised view of themselves in the love partner. When people tell another their 'life story', it is an account that has within it the way they wish to be seen, as well (perhaps) as a real desire to be known by the other person.

Associated with being at one's best, idealised love is an unstable structure, since the worst (one's 'sharpe North' and 'declining West') has been left out of the picture – but has not in fact gone away.

When there is an idealisation, it means that criticisms, doubts and hostilities are kept at bay and are often taken to belong to someone else. A male patient, for example, told me that *all* was well between his wife and himself, the problem was just that their child was so unpleasant and obstructive. The fact that destructiveness and anger are kept at bay, and in this case located in the child, can result in paranoid feelings and beliefs that something is going to come in from outside the relationship and spoil or destroy things, as the patient's child was felt to do.

Idealisation is a part of the state of mind that Klein called the Paranoid Schizoid Position.[17] She thought this was the earliest state of mind in the infant, and one that can recur throughout life, particularly when one is faced with a new situation. In this state of mind, Klein argues, love and hate are kept separate from each other. The split which occurs between love and hate gives some order to the baby's chaos of feelings and protects what is good, enabling it to grow.

An example of such a split between love and hate is given by Meg Harris Williams and Donald Meltzer[18], who suggest that an infant may locate opposite feelings in different places in relation to mother's body. The loving feelings may be located in mother's skin – which can be touched, stroked and experienced as beautiful. The hateful feelings may be located in her insides, which become an ugly place of violence and damage. Perhaps Ted Hughes had such feelings in mind when he drafted the following:

. . . Those are not dogs
That seem to be dogs
Pulling at her. Remember the lean hound
Running up the lane holding high
The dangling raw windpipe and lungs
Of a fox? Now see who
Will drop on all fours at the end of the street
And come romping towards your mother,
Pulling her remains, with their lips . . .[19]

(Ted Hughes, 'The Dogs Are Eating Your Mother')

The fear that one cannot manage hostile

feelings or put right damage done can prevent a person from being free to know about their hostile or destructive feelings at all. If, however, a person has the belief that good will prevail, it makes him or her better able to face the destructiveness that may also be present.

A Complex and Generous Love

One of Melanie Klein's papers, written in the 1920s, begins with a description of the opera *The Magic Word*.[20] The stage opens on a child of six sitting with his homework. He does not want to do it and is rude to his mother. She responds that he will have dry bread and no sugar in his tea as punishment. At this added frustration, the child flies into a rage and smashes things in the room. There is a squirrel in a cage and he tries to stab it with his pen. The squirrel escapes through the window. He opens the grandfather clock and pulls out the copper pendulum. Then the objects he has mistreated come to life and attack him back.

The chair refuses to let him sit down, the stove spits sparks at him. A sad tune is played by the shepherd on the wallpaper who was separated from his loved one when the child ripped the piece down between them.

The child collapses and flees out of doors. There he finds more terror. The insects fight and a tree-trunk bleeds sap. In a dispute about who should get to attack the child first, a squirrel is wounded and falls to the floor. This time, instead of fighting or running away, the child stops and binds the squirrel's paw. As he does so, he whispers 'Mama'. All the animals then stop fighting and whisper 'Mama' too.

When Klein read an account of the opera, she saw more than an explosion of frustration and anger from the child. What, she asks, is being attacked by the child? She concludes that it is the parents in their relationship to each other: the shepherd and the shepherdess are torn apart from each other, the squirrel in the cage is attacked, the pendulum torn from the clock. There is to be nothing inside something else – no penis inside mother's body.

Klein argues that the retaliation from the damaged objects portrays the anxiety that one's attacks will be returned upon oneself in a magnified and terrifying way. This can lead to more violence or a flight from the scene, but the child does neither. What is it that allows the child to break the vicious cycle by caring for the squirrel? The child seems to have found within himself a capacity for concern and a belief that he can put things right. The child 'has learnt to love and believes in love'.[21]

The child's concern for the squirrel is the complex and generous love that belongs to what Klein calls the Depressive Position[22]. By 'position', Klein means the way that the whole of a person's personality is orientated at a particular moment in time, including their anxieties and defences against these. Klein thought that the Depressive Position emerges from the Paranoid Schizoid Position when infants become able to realise that the mother they love and idealise is the same person as the mother they hate and fear. The infant's concern is then that the loved person will have been damaged, perhaps irrevocably, by his or her attacks – the anxiety that mother's insides really have gone to the dogs.

In the earliest Paranoid Schizoid Position, the main anxiety is the survival of the self. Destructiveness is turned outwards to protect the self. In the Depressive Position, the main worry is for the other, the child's worry for the injured squirrel. At first sight, depression would not seem to have much to do with love. Klein, however, thought that *love has to take destructiveness into account*. The capacity to tolerate guilt, without getting too paranoid or overwhelmed by the guilt, is the basis of concern – without which, the notion of enduring love is meaningless. Segal,[23] for example, argues that sustainable peace can follow war only if winner and loser alike can take seriously the amount of damage done and feel guilt at the waste of life and resources. If not, one enemy is replaced by another in a repetitive cycle.

If the child is so frightened by the possibility of irrevocable damage that damage cannot be thought about at all, the child loses the opportunity to check his or her fear of damage against mother's actual state, or to discover a capacity to make reparation. Instead, one might see a rigid denial and idealisation in which everything *has* to be alright or, for example, a 'manic' reparation in which the person rushes around blindly doing good without knowing what is feared to be damaged.

Eros as Putting Something (Back) Together

In his concept of Eros, Freud's interest and attention is in the binding of different elements together; Klein's is in putting something damaged back together (reparation). One important form of reparation is the putting together of a picture about what has happened. Even if the damage (i.e. to the mother or father, represented by the squirrel above) has been done in phantasy, it is real psychically, although not necessarily materially. Reassurance that it is not real does not work on such fears. It may give a temporary relief, but the fear remains. For the person concerned, the wish to destroy has paradoxically to be accepted in all its awfulness (as if mother is actually destroyed) before reparation can be meaningful. Reparation can also involve the recognition that in external reality the damage cannot be put right.

A Concluding Note on Love

Love can feel simple. From a psychoanalytic view, this simplicity is seen as the outcome of a complex intercourse that is going well. By contrast, idealistic love (or denigratory hate) of the other person can, if rigid, result in a simplistic and repetitive kind of relationship.

Something similar can be seen in relation to Eros in the mind, where the capacity to grasp the complexity of a situation can issue in a simple end-idea, whilst the use of rigid, simplistic assumptions can mean that views get repeated without an openness to discovering anything new.

Eros in the Mind: What is Imagination?

Imaginative work is an intercourse between one's internal life and the world around us.

One view of imagination is that it is an activity in which one can think anything one likes, where there is limitless freedom but at the same time inconsequential freedom – inconsequential because it is not connected to reality and therefore not able to make any real difference. Another view, and my view, is that imagination is connected both to a person's inner world and to external reality. From a psychoanalytic point of view, the capacity to be imaginative is to do with the capacity to let oneself be affected. This involves a willingness to be in touch with one's psychic reality and to be affected through an interchange with the world around one, with external reality. One often does not choose what one is going to be affected by and cannot prejudge the outcome.

Imaginative activity may be more obviously linked to artistic work, but it is also integral to making logical hypotheses of the kind, 'If X happens, then Y will happen.' Segal[24] illustrates this point with examples from science-fiction writing and contrasts the 'as if' quality of 'space opera' (an escapist world of heroes and heroines, like daydreams) with science-fiction stories that imagine what would happen if a current parameter were to be changed, such as 'what if' there were no gravity.

In what follows, I am going to look at two

points in people's lives that seem of particular importance to the development of the capacity to be imaginative. One is very early in life. The second is what has been called 'the midlife crisis'.

In the depths of one's mind, one probably never gives up being omnipotent. Somewhere in one's mind, that is, one never gives up believing that one knows everything or is capable of knowing everything, that one is the best and will live forever. In contrast to this, imagination is perhaps most liberated at those moments when one becomes aware of what one does not know or does not have. This is the case in my two examples. Firstly, the baby . . .

The Origins of Imagination

Imagination is necessary to our thinking about things when they are not there and our thought about them when they are.[25]

(Mary Warnock, philosopher)

A baby starts to get hungry and becomes fretful. It then begins to make sucking movements with its mouth and seems to settle down into a contented state. After a few minutes, it breaks down into cries. What happened in the few minutes of contentment? The baby was probably hallucinating the breast. It believed it was feeding – until hunger pangs broke through the hallucination.

Hallucination is an ancestor of daydreams. In both, people try to give themselves what they want and, in particular, try to gratify and soothe themselves. When this breaks down, what happens? The baby may not realise he or she has been hallucinating. The hunger pains may instead be experienced as a 'bad' hallucination of being attacked by a cruel presence.

In hallucination, the baby manufactures its own world; as it gets more in touch with reality, the two are put together. Imagination is where the capacity to manufacture our own world meets up with reality. In particular, as the psychoanalyst Wilfred Bion suggests, it is the discovery of absence which enables the first imaginative thought – the baby who can endure and know the reality of mother's absence can also imagine her in her absence.[26]

Imaginative Creativity and the Mid-life Crisis

Whoever does not, sometime or other, give his full consent . . . to the dreadfulness of life, can never take possession of the unutterable abundance and power of our existence: can only walk on its edge, and one day, when the judgement is given, will have been neither alive nor dead.[27]

In his paper 'Death and the Mid-life Crisis', Jaques suggests that a critical phase in the development of the individual occurs around the age of 35. Jaques took a random sample of some 310 painters, composers, poets, writers and sculptors of greatness. He found that, in comparison to the rest of the population, more of them died in their mid-30s. He makes a link to 'the mid-life crisis', implying that some of these creative people were not able to find a way through it. With less intensity perhaps, it is a crisis that assails everyone when faced with the limitation of what they have achieved and the now visible end of their life. If a person arrives in mid-life without having been able to face some complexity of feeling (including destructive feelings), he or she has limited tools with which to face the mid-life crisis. This, Jaques suggests, can lead to an increased emphasis on appearance, and insistence that all is fine and nothing is changing:

The compulsive attempts, in many men and women reaching middle age, to remain young, the hypochondriacal concern over health and appearance, the emergence of sexual promis-

cuity in order to prove youth and potency, the hollowness and lack of genuine enjoyment of life, and the frequency of religious concern, are familiar patterns.[28]

If, however, one can entertain thoughts about the limits of life, it can deepen one's own experience and respect for other people's lives.

Jaques suggests that when hate, destruction and death are found in youthful art, they tend to take the form of the satanic or the macabre. Whilst in those artists who have been able to endure the crisis, the elements of hate, destruction and death have a more tragic and integrated place in their work. If, by contrast, the artist is not able to get through the crisis, one can see an impoverishment of imaginative activity and its replacement by something more conservative and repetitive.

Wordsworth went through a change in mid-life, both politically and poetically, from being a revolutionary and an innovator to becoming the established and conformist Poet Laureate. Ronald Britton notes that Wordsworth had an unusual capacity in youth to represent loss in his work.[29] In mid-life, Wordsworth took up a more conventional lifestyle. At this point, Britton argues, he seems to have lost the capacity to embrace the periods of upheaval and uncertainty needed if new thought is to be possible. A sense of loss and new realisation is replaced by assertion, coherent belief and moral certainty. Wordsworth, in this view, went on to do good work in his long later life, but his great work was written in his youth.

By contrast to Wordsworth, the work of the contemporary painter Howard Hodgkin is generally accepted to have come to life when he entered his 40s. During this period, Hodgkin left his marriage of 20 years and declared his homosexuality. Andrew Graham-Dixon comments:

If many of the pictures of the first part of his career seem to betray a desire to be elsewhere, the pictures of his later career see that desire fulfilled. They become new and vivid worlds, no longer so sketched around with irony or so often deflected into satire. They are more naked: their colours are raw and the skin of paint that they present to the world becomes increasingly vulnerable, liquid and membranous. They speak of more (more pleasures and predicaments) and they do so more urgently and eloquently.[30]

In a recent article, Hodgkin conveys that the change which occurred in mid-life has continued to the present day. He comments that, although he finds the work more difficult, 'the results are getting ever nearer to what I want'.[31] Hodgkin will be 70 years old in August 2002.

Phantasy and Imagination

He loved her and she loved him
His kisses sucked out her whole past and future
    or tried to
He had no other appetite
She bit him she gnawed him she sucked
She wanted him complete inside her
Safe and Sure forever and ever . . .

His smiles were the garrets of a fairy palace
Where the real world would never come
Her smiles were spider bites
So he would lie still till she felt hungry
His words were occupying armies
Her laughs were an assassin's attempts
His looks were bullets daggers of revenge
Her glances were ghosts in the corner with
    horrible secrets
His whispers were whips and jackboots
Her kisses were lawyers steadily writing . . .

Her vows put his eyes in formalin
At the back of her secret drawer
Their screams stuck in the wall
Their heads fell apart into sleep like the two
*   halves*
Of a lopped melon, but love is hard to stop

In their entwined sleep they exchanged arms
*   and legs*
In their dreams their brains took each other
*   hostage*

In the morning they wore each other's face[32]
                    (Ted Hughes, 'Lovesong')

Hughes' striking poem is the outcome of imaginative work – imaginative work which has a considerable access to phantasy. The poem portrays an intense intercourse on the edge of something sadistic, and one in which the difference between the two people does not return to them in the same form in the morning. On reading it, one has the sense that it is a true picture of such a relationship. It is the imaginative activity which gives a truthful portrait of the relationship – whether the relationship itself is truthful is a different kind of question. By 'truthful portrait' is meant more than accuracy. From a psychoanalytic point of view, it involves other factors too – such as the psychological depth and resonance of what is described.

Phantasy is rather different. I illustrate imaginative work above by Hughes' poem *as a poem* – a composed structure in verse. But phantasy, by contrast, is in the poem and, for example, in the young girl's dream. What then is phantasy?

The psychoanalyst Elizabeth Bott Spillius makes the following point about phantasy:

The word conveys contrasting implications . . . It has a connotation of the imagination and creativity that underlie all thought and feeling, but it also has a connotation of make-believe, a daydream, something that is untrue by the standards of material reality.[33]

An example of the first connotation of the word 'phantasy' (something that underlies all thought and feeling) is the point made earlier that access to infantile phantasies can deepen involvement in an adult relationship and offer some gratification (although unconsciously and not completely) of early desires. Hughes' lovers, for example, know about infantile possessive longings for the other. The second connotation of phantasy – to the fore in daydreams and idealised relations – is more to do with seeing ourselves as we would wish to be. In the world of daydreams and idealised relations, unwelcome qualities or conflicts are located elsewhere. Such 'make-believe' phantasy tends to be fleeting – unless it becomes too addictive *a* – as Hughes says – *fairy palace / Where the real world would never come.*

Although work is done in phantasy – as the young girl works on conflicting feelings in her dream – it is not the same kind of work as happens in imaginative activity. Imaginative thought is more sustained work than phantasy. Whilst it has its roots in phantasy, imaginative thought is where the capacity to manufacture or represent our world meets up with reality. Imaginative work is an intercourse between one's internal and external worlds.

Intercourse in the Mind and Defences Against It

Many psychoanalysts, including Freud and Klein, posit that people are born with what Bion calls 'pre-conceptions'.[34] A pre-conception is a template, enabling us to recognise certain relations when we come across them in our experiences in life. The baby, for example, is born with the expectation of the breast. People are also thought to be born with a template of intercourse; that is, with a kind of pre-knowledge of parental intercourse – the primal scene. Intrinsic to this template is a model of bringing two different things together and Bion, for example, thought a model of intercourse was unconsciously invoked every time we bring things together – in bodies, feelings and ideas. From this point of view, intercourse as a model runs through our lives from birth and is not confined to maturity.

If one's unconscious view is that it is disastrous to let two things come together, then a good deal of energy may go into rigidly ensuring that no thought should interact spontaneously with another. An example of this is a patient who told me, after some time in analysis, that he listened only to the things he thought I was not aware of saying. Anything he felt I wanted to make a point of or showed the slightest pleasure or interest in, he would ignore. He did not give me any 'feedback' about which of my thoughts he had listened to and would not respond to, or elaborate on anything I said. He and I were never to interact in a spontaneous way with one another. His view of intercourse was that of a battleground in which only one of us would prevail. He feared that if he let down his guard, I would take over.

Perverse relations are also a way of avoiding intercourse and difference (separateness). An example of this occurs in the work of the psychoanalyst Betty Joseph. Joseph noted that her patient

. . . was doing something with his fingers . . . He touches the tips of the fingers of one hand against the fingers of the other very softly and almost unceasingly . . . This masturbatory activity seems to have something in common with the mental chuntering, the going over and over things in his mind.[35]

The patient probably would not realise that there was anything sexual in his finger movements. In the analytic exploration of this, however, he and Joseph worked out how the touching of the fingers was an action that repeated something about all his relationships. The picture they discovered over time was one in which he could 'touch' a relationship but not consummate it. In his conscious mind, he knew he was detached from his wife and his analyst, but had not been conscious that this detachment expressed a fear of closeness. In the touching of skin to skin, Joseph and her patient saw a picture in which there was no real separation from the other person – and no real intercourse either.

It may seem odd to derive a sexual meaning from such an innocuous, apparently trivial, action – the touching of the fingers. However, we are familiar with hand gestures that have a sexual meaning. We know about the socially shared, common ones, such as the single-fingered 'up-yours'. Joseph's example is of an action that is more subtle and private.

Simplistic Assumption or Imaginative Simplicity

Freud thought that 'life instinct', or Eros, united different elements to produce ever more complex forms. Imagination is interesting in this context because its relation to complexity is often as a starting point rather than necessarily a complex end-product. I cannot speak for the experience of an artist, but certainly in the psychoanalytic world the most impressive clinicians and theoreticians are those who can take in the complexity of a patient or a problem and then, as a consequence of this, make what can be a simple point. The simple point is the outcome of a capacity to entertain a complicated situation, without 'grasping after certainties'. Bion, who wrote on this subject, was very taken by a letter that Keats wrote to his brother in 1817.

In the letter, Keats speaks of his admiration for writers, particularly Shakespeare, in terms of 'negative capability'. By this, he meant a capacity to stay with what is unknown until new understanding emerges, rather than quickly assume that the new situation is a familiar one.[36]

By contrast, an assumption is a simplistic starting point which is then applied to the data. I need to make a differentiation here between an assumption and a 'pre-conception'. Some of Freud's contemporaries and many others since, for example, have made arguments that imply Freud's theory of sexuality operates like an assumption: i.e., he thought (or assumed) sex was everywhere and so he saw sex everywhere. Psychoanalysts, as well as philosophers, have worked on the problem of circular arguments. The work of Bion on 'pre-conceptions' is particularly useful in this context. Bion argued that theory should be held in the analyst's mind as a 'pre-conception'. By this, he meant the use of a theory to help recognise what material might be, rather than a theory used to impose a premature meaning on it. A pre-conception would, for example, be what a psychoanalyst knows about rivalry. This could help the analyst recognise rivalry in the patient's material and draw on psychoanalytic theory to understand it. (It is always messier than this in practice.) An assumption would occur if it was presumed that whenever the analyst heard about brothers and sisters, for example, the material would necessarily be to do with rivalry. It is a constant struggle for the psychoanalyst to try to minimise the number of assumptions being made.

Assumptions are interesting things in their own right, particularly in the context of Eros. Assumptions can look like the binding activity of Eros, but if rigidly held are actually a deadening force when it comes to thinking. One reason for this, mentioned earlier, is that assumptions ignore any evidence that does not fit, and, because of this, can only be repetitive rather than explorative.

Conclusion

I have suggested that the idea of Eros can illuminate some aspects of sexual intimacy, love and imaginative activity. We can now draw out some of the qualities that the three areas have in common.

- Relations between people and within oneself can have greater fluidity and complexity if destructive impulses are taken into account. From this point of view, feeling alive (Eros) involves one's love and hate.
- Pivotal to having a life of one's own is the recognition of difference and sometimes absence and exclusion.
- Once difference is recognised, there arises the possibility of intercourse. Sexual, emotional and imaginative intercourse are

key vehicles of Eros. Procreation preserves the species. Intercourse is also a model for the interaction between two 'foreign' elements (people, ideas, etc.) that can lead to something new.

- In some circumstances at least, the more complex a grasp one has of a situation, the more alive the outcome. This has been contrasted with the application of assumptions which either limit or exclude genuine imagination.

- One way of seeing whether something is on the side of Eros (life instinct) or Thanatos (death instinct) is by looking at what it does or does not lead to. Does an understanding, for example, lead to further thought or does it close it down? In love, does one want to know more about the other person, or is the relationship to be ended when the other steps outside one's preferred view of them? In sexual relationships, is there a developing intimacy between two people, or is there the absence of interest and concern?

In this essay, we have seen how the force of Eros 'binds together' the strands of our human existence – physically through sex, emotionally through love and mentally through imagination. The 'paradox' of Eros is that this 'aliveness' is not a settled state or a drive to homogeneity, but involves the disruption of an intercourse between 'vitally different' aspects of oneself, other people, experiences or ideas.

Further Reading

Freud's concept of Eros has not been much explored in a direct way. There is a widely held misconception that Freud's Eros was exclusively sexual, but in fact it is a more general principle about a life-giving drive towards intercourse and complexity. In this book, I have included Freud's work and recent developments in psychoanalytic thought.

The Beginning of Eros in Psychoanalytic Thought

'Beyond the Pleasure Principle' is the key text in relation to Eros and psychoanalytic thought. It is a rather uncharacteristic work for Freud, full as it is of biology, but it is far-reaching and seminal to his thinking about what it is to be alive.

In 'The Ego and the Id', Freud develops the ideas started in what he calls his 'Beyond'. This is written without the biology and may be easier to read.

Freud, S., 'Beyond the Pleasure Principle' (1920), in *Standard Edition of the Complete Psychological Works of Sigmund Freud* (hereafter *SE*), vol. 18, London: Hogarth Press, 1953–73.

—— 'The Ego and the Id' (1923), in *SE*, vol. 19.

Of Eros in the Body: Sexuality

I read quite widely the English language texts on Sexuality when writing *Eros* and found, perhaps unsurprisingly, that the most open-minded, comprehensive and insightful text was Freud's 'Three Essays'. If it has been bettered, I have not found it.

A belief in the contemporary psychoanalytic world is that British psychoanalysts, and in particular British Kleinian psychoanalysts, do not pay attention to sexuality, whilst French psychoanalysts do. There is certainly less published work about adult sexuality in British psychoanalysis, although this may not reflect clinical practice. French psychoanalyst André Green has written evocatively on Eros for those who wish to pursue the topic further.

Texts that refer specifically to the Oedipus complex include Freud's *Interpretation of Dreams* and Ronald Britton's contemporary *Belief and Imagination*.

Freud, S., 'Three Essays on the Theory of Sexuality' (1905), in *SE*, vol. 7.

—— *The Interpretation of Dreams* (1900), in *SE*, vols. 4 and 5.

Green, A., *Chains of Eros* (1997), London: Rebus Press, 2000.

Britton, R., *Belief and Imagination*, London: Routledge, 1998.

Of Eros in the Emotions: Love

Melanie Klein is perhaps particularly known for her work on the death instinct and aggression, but she is also responsible for some of the most innovative work on love. She does not link her work directly to Freud's concept of Eros but it fits well with it. A good place to start is Klein's papers in the *Selected Melanie Klein*, ed. by Mitchell. If one wants to go on from there, Klein's work is collected in four volumes.

Hanna Segal is an eminent contemporary psychoanalyst and the author of a lucid and profound account of Klein's work. Her collection of essays, *Psychoanalysis, Literature and War*, contains a paper on war and peace which builds on Klein's work on love.

Klein, M., *The Selected Melanie Klein*, ed. Juliet Mitchell, London: Penguin Books, 1986.

——*Collected Works of Melanie Klein*, London: Hogarth Press and Institute of Psychoanalysis, 1975. Vol. I: *Love, Guilt and Reparation, and Other Works*; Vol. II:

The Psycho-Analysis of Children; Vol. III: *Envy and Gratitude, and Other Works*; Vol. IV: *Narrative of a Child Analysis*.

Segal, H., *Klein*, London: Karnac, 1989.

——*Psychoanalysis, Literature and War*, ed. John Steiner, London: Routledge, 1997.

Of Eros in the Mind: Imagination

Wilfred Bion is a central figure in this area. My suggestion would be to start with *Second Thoughts*, although a colleague, David Bell, suggests *Learning from Experience*. I give both references below. The work of Bion specifically referred to in the text includes the last of a group of four books: *Learning from Experience*, *Elements of Psychoanalysis*, *Transformations* and *Attention and Interpretation*. *Attention and Interpretation* has had a considerable effect on psychoanalysis but would not, I think, be the best place to start.

Ronald Britton's book is a clear and thought-provoking contemporary Kleinian exposition of psychoanalytic ways of thinking about the mind.

Betty Joseph's writing is intensely clinical and her approach gives us an innovative development of Bion's work.

Elizabeth Bott Spillius's paper on phantasy explores complex ideas relevant to imaginative thought in an accessible way.

Bion, W., *Second Thoughts: Selected Papers on Psychoanalysis* (1967), London: Karnac, 1984.

——*Learning from Experience* (1962), London: Karnac, 1984.

——*Attention and Interpretation* (1970), London: Karnac, 1984.

Britton, R., *Belief and Imagination*, London: Routledge, 1998.

Joseph, B., *Psychic Equilibrium and Psychic Change*, ed. Elizabeth Bott Spillius and Michael Feldman, London: Routledge, 1989.

Spillius, E., 'Freud and Klein on the Concept of Phantasy', *International Journal of Psycho-Analysis*, vol. 82, part 2, April 2001, pp. 361–75.

The references I have given are not exhaustive. The majority of authors in the list are from the Kleinian tradition. In privileging textual coherence, I am aware that I have not dealt with much interesting work from the Independent and Contemporary Freudian analytic traditions in Britain.

Literary References

Adams, T., 'It's the Vision Thing', *The Observer Review*, 10 June 2001.

Donne, J. (1572–1631), 'The Good-Morrow', in *The Nation's Favourite Love Poems*, ed. D. Goodwin, London: Penguin, 1997, p. 73.

Graham-Dixon, A., *Howard Hodgkin*, London: Thames and Hudson, 1994.

Hughes, T., 'Lovesong', in *Crow: From the Life and Songs of the Crow*, London: Faber and Faber, 1970.

—— 'The Dogs are Eating Your Mother', in *Birthday Letters*, London: Faber and Faber, 1998.

Rilke, R.M., 'Duino Elegies', in *The Selected Poetry of Rainer Maria Rilke*, ed. and trans. S. Mitchell, London: Pan Books, 1987.

About the Front Cover

Rembrandt's *Danaë* on the front cover was recommended by the Publishing Director of Icon Books, Jeremy Cox. Art historian Mariët Westermann gives an account of the painting in her book on Rembrandt:

The princess Danaë was locked into a bronze chamber by her father, because an oracle had foretold that she would give birth to his future killer. Inflamed with lust for her, Jupiter changed himself into a shower of gold and entered her room through the window. Almost all artists presented Jupiter in the form of gold coins, a fitting bribe for Danaë's elderly female guard or the maiden herself. Rembrandt's rare decision to picture the god as sunlight is more plausible, for light passes through glass . . . Although Artists had often interpreted Danaë as a model of chastity, her Venetian Venus pose and the small Cupid suspended above her head emphasise Danaë's delight at the unexpected turn of events. Soon, when Jupiter and Danaë consummate their love, Venus's son may shed his manacles and cease his weeping. The gilded Cupid and the bed ornamented in the fashionable 'auricular' style, turn Danaë's bronze prison into a sumptuous venue for a tryst.

(pp. 121–2)

It is of note that the painting was attacked with sulphuric acid in 1985. This severely corroded Danaë's legs, arms and head, and the painting is now beyond repair.

Mariët Westermann, *Rembrandt*, London: Phaidon Press, 2000.

Notes

1. 'The analogy of our two basic instincts extends from the sphere of living things to the pair of opposing forces – attraction and repulsion – which rule in the inorganic world.' Sigmund Freud, 'An Outline of Psycho-Analysis' (1940 [1938]) in *Standard Edition of the Complete Psychological Works of Sigmund Freud* (hereafter *SE*), vol. 23, London: Hogarth Press, 1953–73, p. 149.

2. Elizabeth Bott Spillius's thought on the nature of difference is drawn on throughout the book.

3. Sigmund Freud, 'Beyond the Pleasure Principle' (1920), in *SE*, vol. 18, p. 50.

4. Sigmund Freud, 'The Libido Theory' (1923 [1922]), in *SE*, vol. 18, p. 258.

5. Sigmund Freud, 'The Ego and the Id' (1923), in *SE*, vol. 19, p. 40.

6. Sigmund Freud, 'Beyond the Pleasure Principle', op. cit., p. 55 (my emphasis).

7. See Sigmund Freud, 'Beyond the Pleasure Principle', op. cit.

8. Sigmund Freud, 'The Libido Theory', op. cit., p. 258.

9. Sigmund Freud, 'Three Essays on the Theory of Sexuality' (1905), in *SE*, vol. 7.

10. James George Frazer (trans.), *Apollodorus: The Library*, 3.5.7–9 (Loeb Classical Library),

Cambridge, MA: Harvard University Press, 1921, pp. 343–51. Quoted in Lowell Edmunds, *Oedipus: The Ancient Legend and Its Later Analogues*, Baltimore, MD: Johns Hopkins University Press, 1985, p. 52.

11. For texts in which Freud explores this issue in relation to himself, see: Sigmund Freud, *The Interpretation of Dreams* (1900), *SE*, vol. 4; and Jeffrey Masson (ed.), *The Complete Letters of Sigmund Freud to Wilhelm Fliess: 1887–1904*, Cambridge, MA: Harvard University Press, 1985.

12. Ronald Britton, 'Getting in on the Act: The Hysterical Solution', in *International Journal of Psycho-Analysis*, vol. 80, part 1, February 1999, pp. 1–15.

13. Henri Ellenberger, 'The Story of "Anna O": A Critical Review with New Data' (1993), in *Beyond the Unconscious: Essays of Henri F. Ellenberger in the History of Psychiatry*, ed. Mark S. Micale, trans. Françoise Dubor, Princeton, NJ: Princeton University Press, 1993, pp. 254–72.

14. Peter Gay, *Freud: A Life for Our Time*, London and Melbourne: J.M. Dent, 1988, pp. 66–7. Quoted by Ronald Britton, op. cit., p. 7.

15. John Donne (1572–1631), 'The Good-Morrow', in *The Nation's Favourite Love Poems*, ed. Daisy Goodwin, London: Penguin, 1997, p. 73.

16. William Congreve, *The Old Bachelor* (1693), act 4, sc. 7, in *The Oxford Dictionary of Quotations: New Edition*, ed. Angela Partington, London: BCA by arrangement with OUP, 1992, p. 215.

17. Melanie Klein, 'Notes on Some Schizoid Mechanisms' (1946), in *The Selected Melanie Klein*, ed. Juliet Mitchell, London: Penguin Books, 1986.

18. Donald Meltzer and Meg Harris Williams, *The Apprehension of Beauty: The Role of Aesthetic Conflict in Development, Art and Violence*, Old Ballechin, Strath Tay: Clunie, 1988.

19. Ted Hughes, 'The Dogs Are Eating Your Mother', in *Birthday Letters*, London: Faber and Faber, 1998, p. 195, reproduced by kind permission of the Ted Hughes Estate and Faber and Faber. This poem, addressed to Frieda and Nicholas – Ted Hughes' and Sylvia Plath's children – concerns their mother's suicide and is intended to explore how the children can recover both themselves and their mother's spirit.

20. Melanie Klein, 'Infantile Anxiety Situations Reflected in a Work of Art and in the Creative Impulse' (1929), in Juliet Mitchell (ed.), op. cit.

21. Ibid., p. 89.

22. Melanie Klein, 'Mourning and Its Relation to Manic-Depressive States' (1940), in Juliet Mitchell (ed.), op. cit.

23. Hanna Segal, 'From Hiroshima to the Gulf War and After: Socio-political Expressions of Ambivalence', in John Steiner (ed.), *Psychoanalysis, Literature and War: Papers 1972–95*, London: Routledge, 1997, pp. 157–69.

24. Hanna Segal, *Dream, Phantasy and Art*, London: Routledge, 1991. See Chapter 8, 'Imagination, Play and Art'.

25. Mary Warnock, *Imagination*, London: Faber and Faber, 1976, p. 12.

26. Wilfred Bion, 'A Theory of Thinking', *International Journal of Psycho-Analysis*, vol. 43, parts 4–5, 1962; reprinted in Wilfred Bion, *Second Thoughts: Selected Papers on Psychoanalysis*, London: Karnac, 1984, pp. 110–20.

27. Rainer Maria Rilke, 'Letter to Countess Margot Sizzo-Noris-Crouy' (12 April 1923), concerning her poem 'Duino Elegies', in *The Selected Poetry of Rainer Maria Rilke*, ed. and trans. S. Mitchell, London: Pan Books, 1987, p. 317. Quoted by Ronald Britton, *Belief and Imagination*, London: Routledge, 1998, p. 165.

28. Elliott Jaques, 'Death and the Mid-life Crisis' (1965), in Elizabeth Bott Spillius (ed.), *Melanie Klein Today: Volume 2: Mainly Practice*, London: Routledge, 1988, pp. 226–49.

29. Ronald Britton, *Belief and Imagination*, London: Routledge, 1998. See Chapter 11, 'Wordsworth: The Loss of Presence and the Presence of Loss'.

30. Andrew Graham-Dixon, *Howard Hodgkin*, London: Thames and Hudson, 1994, p. 21.

31. Howard Hodgkin, quoted by Tim Adams, 'It's the Vision Thing', *The Observer Review*, 10 June 2001.

32. Ted Hughes, 'Lovesong', in *Crow: From the Life and Songs of the Crow*, London: Faber and Faber, 1970, reproduced by kind permission of the Ted Hughes Estate and Faber and Faber. 'Lovesong' is part of a longer story – 'The Story of Crow'. Crow reaches a river he needs to cross if he is to reach Happy Land, where he believes his bride awaits him. At the river, a hag demands that he carry her across. As he does so, she gets heavier and heavier, pushing him down into the gravel on the river bed, until only his head is above water. She questions him and demands he sing the answer. When he gets part of it right she gets lighter, when wrong she gets heavier. She asks him seven questions: 'The questions change. They begin at the negative extreme and end at the positive. The first question expects the darkest answer. "Who paid most, him or her?" Crow's answer is "Lovesong".' (Keith Sagar, 'The Story of Crow', in

The Laughter of Foxes: A Study of Ted Hughes, Liverpool: Liverpool University Press, 2000, p. 179.)

33. Elizabeth Bott Spillius, 'Freud and Klein on the Concept of Phantasy', *International Journal of Psycho-Analysis*, vol. 82, part 2, April 2001, pp. 361–75 (p. 362).

34. Wilfred Bion, op. cit.

35. Betty Joseph, 'Addiction to Near-death' (1982), in *Psychic Equilibrium and Psychic Change*, ed. Elizabeth Bott Spillius and Michael Feldman, London: Routledge, 1989, pp. 127–39.

36. Wilfred Bion, *Attention and Interpretation*, London: Tavistock, 1970; reprinted London: Karnac, 1984, p. 125.

Dedication

To Eric, Hannah and Naomi

Acknowledgements

My thanks to my patients. I also want to thank Elizabeth Bott Spillius, Betty Joseph, Maggie Mills, Ivan Ward and Penny Woolcock for their support and insight.